HOW POPPY GREW HAPPY

Written and illustrated by K G Subramanyan

Seagull Books

CALCUTTA, 2019

First published in 1979 at the Fine Arts Fair
by the Graphic Art Department,
Faculty of Fine Arts, M. S. University of Baroda.

Seagull Books, 2008
Second printing, 2019

ISBN 978 8 1704 6 286 6

Published by Naveen Kishore
Seagull Books Private Limited
36C, S.P. Mukherjee Road, Calcutta 700 025

Typeset by Seagull Books, Calcutta, India
Printed and bound by Hyam Enterprises, Calcutta, India

Though it was
a fine day,
Poppy felt mopy.

So a sparrow came
and sat near her
and said, Chirrup.

What? asked Poppy crossly.

I said, cheer up,
said the sparrow.

What is there
to cheer up for?
said Poppy in anger.
Pop went to office without
giving me a pat.

And Mom forced
me to drink

that gooey glass
of milk.

She was in tears.

The sparrow chuckled and said, Is that something to mope about?

There are lots of things on such a day to feel nice about. Come out and I will show you.

But before that
put a neat smile on.

But how?
whined Poppy.

This is how,
showed the sparrow.

We are dull birds,
said the sparrow,
But I will
show you some
far prettier
than us.

Then he showed
a parrot.
Is that a parrot!
marvelled Poppy.

She looks so much
like Mom.

With all that
green silk and red lips.

Then the sparrow
showed her a peacock.
All set with sequins
he seemed.

Is he dressed up
for a wedding?
asked Poppy.

Then the sparrow showed the butterflies.
White streaked with yellow. Red circled with blue.
Black chequered with orange.

They were bright and playful. And always on the move. Now in the air, now on the flower. Now near, now so far away.

Then she came
to the flowers.

The bushy roses.
The gaudy canna.
The drooping dahlias.

And she gasped
with pleasure.

Then saw the squirrel
in the shade.

Squirrey, Squirrey,
she called and
ran after them.

The squirrel
was too quick.

He ran up a tree
with his tail
in the air.

Then he wiggled
his nose at her.

Poppy laughed.
Poppy was happy.

She forgot her blues.
She forgot even
the sparrow.